HOW TO WORK

LIKE A CAT

HOW TO WORK

LIKE A **CAT**

Walking With Confidence
Through a **Dog-Eat-Dog** World

Karen Wormald

WILLOW CREEK PRESS

To my faithful, furry colleagues…Fred, Yul, and Adele.
And in loving memory of …Coco, Cleo, Rex, and Ginger

Published by Willow Creek Press
P.O. Box 147, Minocqua, Wisconsin 54548

Photo Credits:
AnimalsAnimals: page 2 © Robert Pearcy; page 56 © Michael Gadomski; page 67 © Ulrike Schanz; pages 68, 91 © J. & P. Wegner;
Ardea.com: pages 12, 27, 51, 88 © John Daniels; page 33 © Jean Michel Labat
Click the Photo Connection: pages 8, 16, 44, 52, 60, 80, 92 © Diane Calkins; page 28 © Rosemary Shelton;
© Cris Kelly: pages 11, 71
© Kent Dannen: pages 35, 48
© Frank S. Balthis; page 31, 96
Peter Arnold, Inc.: pages 47, 59 © PHONE Labat Jean-Michel; page 80 © BIOS Gunther Michel;
ronkimballstock.com: page 15 © Renee Stockdale; pages 23, 24 55, 79, 84 © Ron Kimball;
page 43 © Mark McQueen
Superstock: page 7 © Mauritius; pages 39, 63 © J Silver; pages 40, 64 © age fotostock; page 75 © George Goodwin;
© Terry Wild Studio, Inc. pages 19, 20 72
© Norvia Behling: page 76
© Wendy Shattil/Bob Rozinski: page 32
© Paulette Braun: page 87

Design: Donnie Rubo
Printed in Canada

Introduction

In most jobs, you're expected to work like a dog... Show boundless enthusiasm for any dull and pointless task; act thrilled with any meager reward that's tossed your way; play nice with the other dogs; and never question the leader of the pack. For your own sanity, you need to wise up and end this ridiculous canine charade.

Cats have it all figured out. They live by their own rules. They refuse to be herded. They're self-assured and serene; they're imaginative; and they're not afraid to take daring leaps.

If you work like a cat, you'll find that drudgery isn't its own reward—a catnap is. You'll shed meaningless activities, and you'll assert your natural superiority over incompetent, annoying co-workers.

Once you break free of the leash, your potential for greatness is unlimited. Remember, no cat ever hesitated to climb a tree because it was too tall. Good luck!

Refuse to be just a ball of fur in the crowd.

Dogs love to pull sleds in packs. Frank Sinatra loved being the leader of his world-famous Rat Pack. But in the entire history of civilization, there's never been a cat pack. Don't be afraid to make like the cheese in the children's song and stand alone. It's much easier to have your accomplishments noticed when no one's hanging onto your tail.

6

Don't compromise your hygiene to get ahead.

Dogs may think butt sniffing is the key to achieving greatness, but they can't see where they're going with their faces buried in someone else's backside. Cats don't showcase their innumerable skills and talents by posing with their noses stuck in unpleasant places. Remember, the only tail you ever need to lick is your own.

If you ever experience moments of uncertainty, remind yourself that dogs think the world is a bathroom.

When it comes to being misguided and clueless, dogs are unmatched. Even canines with impeccable pedigrees think it's perfectly OK to leave a nasty mess anywhere for others to step in. Cats, with their innate grace, dignity, poise, intelligence, and modesty, have no reason to feel inferior to any species under any circumstances.

When you're not around, don't expect to get any work out of the mice.

In addition to dogs, you'll encounter many meek little rodents who need constant monitoring and guidance from someone who will handle them with a firm paw. Throughout the ages, if mice had ever presented any threat to cats, they wouldn't be portrayed as feckless losers in quaint old sayings.

If you find yourself surrounded by a pack, exploit its need for a leader.

Most dogs suffer from low self-esteem and prefer to be dominated. If the opportunity presents itself, step in and oblige them. Assign them to do all your fetching. They'll be so grateful for the chance to look busy and impress the boss, they'll forget they should be chasing you, not serving you.

It's a myth that curiosity kills the cat—boredom does.

To keep the bounce in your step, don't let your surroundings become so familiar that they cease to challenge you. Collect some intriguing trinkets, stash them in out-of-the-way places, and forget them. One day when you need inspiration or you don't have anything better to do, you'll have delightful diversions waiting for you.

Fortunately, cats rarely get bored.

A cat's greatest enemy is the status quo. You must never lose your willingness to poke around in places you've never explored before. Maybe you'll only end up with a paw-ful of cobwebs for your trouble, but you'll never uncover a lost and forgotten hoard of treats if you never bother to look for it.

COMPANY
DOCUMENTS

Don't let anyone rub your fur the wrong way.

It's never acceptable to let yourself be disrespected or mistreated. If someone tries, you have three options:

1) stare at them coldly until they stop;
2) return the favor by inflicting some pain of your own, or
3) walk away. Don't just lie there and take it or you'll be setting yourself up for more abuse.

When everyone else is in a panic, rely on your unflappable feline composure.

There are times when people who need to feel important create a faux crisis. They just want to sit back and watch everyone else chase their tails. However, you should remain still and refuse to participate because some games are best played by ignoring them. That's why cats don't chase Frisbees.

Keep your claws retracted— most of the time.

You possess superior defense—and offense—against all opponents. Preserve the element of surprise by keeping your deadly talons sheathed until you need to use them. If you ever feel compelled to shred something, count to ten first and make sure it's nothing you value because that would be self-defeating.

Never take your eyes off your goal.

Most people let their lives be ruled by myriad petty distractions. Then they whine about never being able to get anything done. As a cat, you are blessed with the patience, focus, and physical stamina to achieve any objective you choose. You always deliver results, not excuses.

When the going gets tough, follow the example of your undomesticated relatives.

Make no mistake—any office is a jungle. It doesn't take much to turn your co-workers into savages. Don't be afraid to roar when you need to be heard above the chaos. Sometimes it takes a big cat's majestic presence to remind everyone what dignified behavior is supposed to look like.

Be in the right place at the right time.

Stake out a special spot to call your own that's warmed by the sun every day. It's the perfect place for power-catnaps. If you take time to unwind, you'll always be perky, playful, and productive and have everyone wondering how you manage it.

Go out of your way to be cordial to those who don't like cats.

Those who believe unsubstantiated myths—like black cats are bad luck—are also suckers for the baloney that dogs are their best friends. Typically, they've just never had a cat bestow on them the honor of its company. You can win these people over by showing empathy and warm, focused attention—the last things they expect from a feline.

Don't be finicky without a good reason.

Some consider a cat's highly discerning nature a negative trait, so don't perpetuate this unflattering stereotype by turning up your nose just to be difficult or to flaunt your power. Save your disdain for things that truly deserve contempt—like Frisbees imprinted with the company logo.

The time you spend on personal grooming is never wasted.

It's impossible not to radiate confidence when your fur is silky and every whisker is in place. A sense of style that seems effortless always makes a lasting positive impression. No one needs to know how long—or where—you had to lick yourself to achieve such perfection.

Hairballs are not meant to be kept inside.

If something is upsetting you, don't hesitate to lay it out on the floor and deal with it while it's fresh, even if it makes a mess. No good ever came from hiding problems under the rug and allowing them to fester. Eventually, someone will come along and uncover them—and the consequences are usually even worse.

Always trust your own whiskers.

When you're faced with an important decision, rely on the facts you can verify. Cat-haters with hidden agendas may try to sway your judgment, but their pathetic games can't compete with the knowledge and experience that comes from living nine lives.

Catfights are best watched from the sidelines.

Engaging in public brawls just makes you look like a scrappy alley cat. When conflict will accomplish nothing but to ruffle everyone's fur, hold your tail high and walk away. Proving yourself right isn't worth the hours of licking it will take to regain your composure and dignity.

Any cat who fakes hairballs is just a drama queen.

Any cat who gets into the bad habit of hacking just to get attention sacrifices the respect she's earned. Then even if she licked herself sick to produce a genuine wad, no one would take it seriously or express sympathy. All you have to do to draw all eyes in your direction is to enter a room, so skip the theatrics.

Given no choice but to attack, be sure to draw blood.

If someone is unwise enough to corner you into a fight, make it memorable so they won't ever come back for more. A good way to do this is to leave a scar. The mark will commemorate the confrontation and serve as a warning to anyone else who might be tempted to trifle with you.

Cat skeletons are never found in trees for a good reason.

Whenever cats find themselves in tough spots, they don't shy from taking bold, immediate action. Because you know you'll always land on your feet—and you have nine lives—go ahead and be daring. You've got nothing to lose.

Don't accept expensive gifts from those who would buy your favor.

But you can let them leave the boxes, bows, and wrapping paper behind. They're usually more fun, anyway.

Always leave your mark—tastefully.

Your natural dignity and class are sure to inspire fond memories of you. Resist the temptation to provide others with more tangible mementos of your encounters, like spraying the wall or etching your monogram into the new mahogany conference table. Such grand, timeless gestures are never properly appreciated.

Don't confuse your tail with your mouth.

Dogs live in a state of frenzy with their incessant tail-wagging. That's why they're frequently sent off in pointless searches for tennis balls, sticks, and dead fowl. Don't follow their example. Indiscriminate posterior action can broadcast emotions best kept to yourself. Use your tail to punctuate your statements, not to make them.

Everyone may want to pet you, but not everyone is your friend.

Your soft fur and stunning good looks may serve to bring you popularity, but don't let it go to your head. There will always be unenlightened souls who think the world would be better off without cats. Share cuddles and behind-the-ear licks only with those who genuinely appreciate you.

Show respect for the operator of the can opener.

It's never wise to alienate anyone who controls your destiny. No one says you have to love everyone with thumbs, since that may be their only advantage over you. But you must learn to tolerate with good humor those in superior positions, even if you'd rather sharpen your claws on them.

When there's nothing brilliant to be said, remain silent.

A cat's gaze is worth a thousand meows. When you're with a pack of howling dogs, stare at the far wall in an air of deep contemplation and wait for them to shut up. All that senseless noise will make your next utterance seem profound in comparison, no matter what you say.

Walk softly and carry a big rodent.

You don't have to flaunt it, but it never hurts to occasionally be seen with your "catch of the day." You'll cement the impression that you don't hesitate to go after what you want—and you always get it.

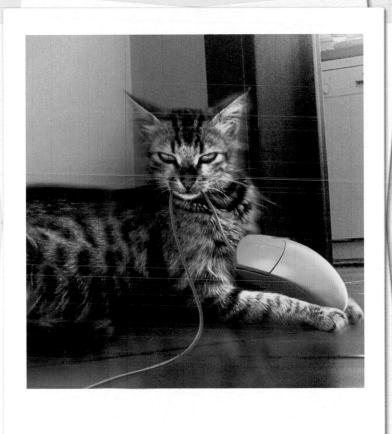

When you can't beat 'em, lick 'em.

You don't have to be a bully to get your way. Just perk up your whiskers, let out a long, rumbling purr, and start licking your target on the nose. They'll do anything you ask, just to get that rough tongue and tuna breath out of their face.

When dining with colleagues, don't be the most finicky one at the table.

Others can't always appreciate a cat's discriminating taste, so it's easy to get yourself unjustifiably labeled "high-maintenance" during business social occasions. Instead, curl up your paws and let someone else run the wait staff ragged with demands. And if the meal is truly awful, fight your natural urge to bury it.

Manage by walking around—anywhere but on the floor.

A great way to survey your domain—and keep others on their toes—is to show up unexpectedly in places no one else can reach. It's even better if they can't figure out how you got there. And never let them see you leave. It's important to maintain that air of omnipotence.

If someone brings a tree into the office during the holidays, refrain from climbing it.

Even if you think there are no witnesses, this is the sort of playful act that will invariably come back to haunt you. You might as well cavort at the next company party with a lampshade on your head. However, feel free to "accidentally" bump a few of the shiny ornaments as you stroll by during the regular course of business.

Decline to serve on any committee whose stated goal is "to build a better mousetrap."

This is guaranteed to be a perfect waste of time. You, of all creatures, know it doesn't take fancy gimmicks to catch mice. However, if someone ever floats the idea of building a cat trap, volunteer to help and then make sure the smarty-pants ends up in the dog house.

Refuse to become a slave to your own popularity.

Unlike dogs, cats couldn't care less if their behavior pleases anyone—even when it does. If you never let yourself become obsessed with trying to be liked, you can do virtually anything you want, make up the rules as you go along, and waste no time listening to criticism.

You don't have to befriend every dog you meet.

Some dogs are naturally more likable than others. Don't bother hanging around the disagreeable ones just to seem like a team player. If the circumstances were reversed, they'd either shun you or chase you when the boss wasn't looking.

To burst some big mutt's pompous bubble, tell a dumb dog joke.

This is a tactic where you do risk offending some dogs who take themselves too seriously—if they get your punchline. But go ahead anyway. You never have to fear retaliation because there's no such thing as a dumb cat joke.

Let sleeping dogs lie.

When they're not barking at nothing, howling at nothing, peeing on everything, or running in aimless circles looking for something to fetch, you can get a lot more work done.

Never let anyone teach you to roll over and play dead.

Leave this trick strictly to the dogs. They think learning how to be a doormat is a marketable job skill. Besides, your days should be filled with more constructive pursuits, like finding the perfect cozy corner for your next power-catnap.

Leap to the top
while everyone else
looks for the ladder.

From a casual stance, cats can easily jump many times their height. Whenever you see a choice opportunity to soar above your competition, don't miss it. If someone yowls, claim you did it for the exercise. But refuse to surrender your lofty new perch and great view.

Never feel threatened by rats.

It was no accident that cats came out on top during the Black Plague. If you notice vermin sneaking around your office, be gracious to any smart ones who try to get along with you—they could prove useful. Flash a tooth and claw to the rest to signal that you'll happily help them join their ancestors from the Middle Ages if they cross you.

If an ambitious young pup proposes, "You scratch my back and I'll scratch yours," try to keep a straight face.

The poor little fellow is getting bad advice from someone, and he obviously doesn't realize he's about to be shredded.

Be prepared for copycats.

Feel flattered when your colleagues notice the fine example you set and try to emulate you. Don't gloat when they fail miserably. They have no way of knowing that, like every cat, your style is unique.

Take time to stop and smell the catnip.

Don't let your job consume your life. If you regularly relax and enjoy the company of friends, family, and pets, you'll be able to tackle your work with the enthusiasm you usually reserve for chasing butterflies. And work may even get to be fun.

You may look like a pussycat, but you're a lion inside.

It's no coincidence that cats are the only creatures blessed with nine lives—their wisdom, talents, and flair transcend the ages. Now it's your turn. Go out there and be great!